BRINGING YOUR STRATEGIC PLAN TO LIFE

BRINGING YOUR STRATEGIC PLAN TO LIFE

A Guide for Nonprofits and Public Agencies

KATHLEEN A. PARIS, PhD

iUniverse, Inc.
Bloomington

Bringing Your Strategic Plan to Life
A Guide for Nonprofits and Public Agencies

iUniverse books may be ordered through booksellers or by contacting:

iUniverse
1663 Liberty Drive
Bloomington, IN 47403
www.iuniverse.com
1-800-Authors (1-800-288-4677)

Cover design by CLC Advertising Design and Artwork

Content: Pt. 1: Design your plan with implementation in mind—Pt. 2. Evaluate your plan to be sure it can be implemented—Pt. 3. Communicate the plan in multiple ways—Pt. 4. Use tools to help implement—Pt. 5. Budget for the plan.

ISBN: 978-1-4620-2785-9 (sc)
ISBN: 978-1-4620-2786-6 (e)

Library of Congress Control Number: 2011913255

1. Strategic planning 2. Execution 3. Nonprofit 4. Public sector 5. Performance excellence 6. Alignment 7. Implementation 8. Budgeting

Printed in the United States of America

iUniverse rev. date: 11/09/2011

Contents

How to Use This Book

I am imagining that, because you are reading this, you have some responsibility for a planning process. While writing *Bringing Your Strategic Plan to Life: A Guide for Nonprofits and Public Agencies,* I was mindful of the hectic pace any decision-maker maintains. My aim was to boil down what I have learned over the past twenty-five years to the most essential activities and suggestions.

No organization needs to carry out every action described here. For example, time spent identifying stakeholder needs (see pp. 10-11) will probably vary directly with the size of the organization.

I suggest reading this book with highlighter in hand, marking those actions that make sense for your organization. You might invite a few others to do the same and then compare notes.

You will notice that there is ample space for you to make your own notes, and there are entry points to find help wherever you currently are in the planning process.

I have included what I consider best practices—activities that have consistently paid off for the groups and organizations with which I have worked. There are many ways to approach planning successfully, and they can look very different in different organizations.

My own "rock bottom" requirement is to involve staff and stakeholders in some way in the planning process. Even if a board or governance body is charged with planning, the reality is that no small group at the top has enough information to make far-reaching choices without input from those who are closer to the action. Conversely, the people carrying out the daily work of the organization do not have the same view of the larger playing field that a board member or elected official may have. Combining these various levels of knowledge helps make a plan realistic and viable.

You can't go wrong if you approach planning as an activity aimed at taking the whole organization or group successfully into the future. If you think of planning that way, it will become a lot more interesting.

What Is Strategic Planning?

Strategic planning is a structured approach to anticipating the future and exploiting the inevitable. It is a means of establishing major directions for an organization and concentrating resources accordingly. The aim is to maximize benefits to stakeholders.

The power of strategic planning is the power of focus. You know how much one individual can get done if that person has a focus, resources, and a deadline. Imagine what an organization can do if everyone in the organization is working toward the same goals!

Why have so many people had disappointing experiences with strategic planning? My thought is that too much time is often spent on the process of creating the plan, and too little time is spent on creating processes and structures for implementation. Also, it's easy to confuse the strategic plan document with planning strategically. Yes, the plan document matters a lot. It's the road map for the organization. The plan should shape how people do their everyday work. In fact, every employee should have a direct line of sight between the work he or she does and the documented priorities of the organization.

Planning, on the other hand, is an ongoing process that requires people in the organization to talk to each other regularly, providing updates on goals achieved or roadblocks experienced. Everyone has to be aware of changes that require new, modified, or more coordinated actions. You will find many tips in this booklet for keeping the plan a living and relevant document.

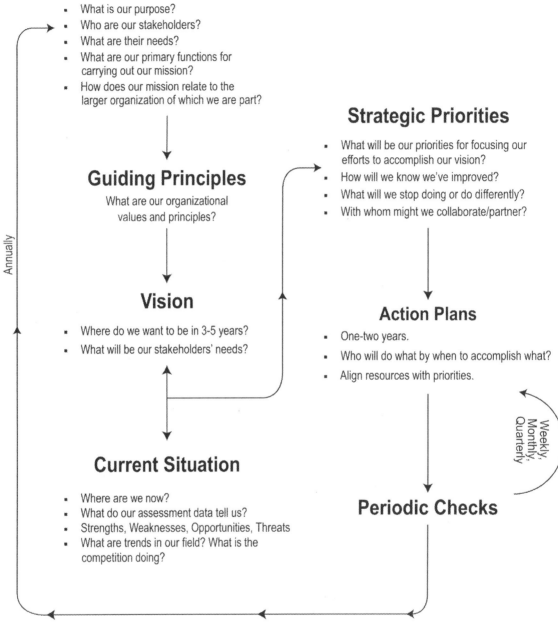

Figure 1. Strategic Planning Model

Adapted and reprinted with permission from the Office of Quality Improvement,
University of Wisconsin-Madison, www.quality.wisc.edu.

A Strategic Planning Process

Any comprehensive plan requires at a minimum these elements: mission, vision, strategic priorities, annual plans, and an implementation system. Various planning models provide a means of identifying mission, vision, and strategic priorities. An adaptation of the excellent model developed by the Office of Quality Improvement at the University of Wisconsin–Madison is shown in Figure 1. The model scales up or down, and the questions are those that any organization needs to ask itself in planning for the future. Other models which may be useful to you are the Strategy Change Cycle developed by Bryson[1] and the Integrated Planning Process created by Below, Morrissey, and Acomb.[2]

Most organizations lose momentum when it comes to actually implementing their plans. This guide is divided into five sections, or dimensions of planning, that need to be considered for an excellent implementation system. The five dimensions include:

1. Creating the plan

2. Evaluating the plan

3. Communicating the plan

4. Implementing the plan

5. Budgeting for the plan

---

[1] John Bryson, *Strategic Planning for Public and Nonprofit Organizations: A Guide to Strengthening and Sustaining Organizational Achievement* (San Francisco: Jossey-Bass, 2004), 33.

[2] Patrick J. Below, George L. Morrissey, and Betty L. Acomb, *The Executive Guide to Strategic Planning* (San Francisco: Jossey-Bass, 1987), 5.

1. Creating the Plan

a. Involve the whole staff in some way. They need to understand the priorities (and the reasons behind them) in order to carry them out well.

Everyone should have an opportunity to be involved in some way, but not everyone needs to be involved in every step.

- See pp. 9-10, *Engaging People in the Planning Process.*

b. Identify a small group (five to twelve people) to serve on the planning committee with multiple ways for many people to have input.

What individuals come to mind as potential members of the planning committee?

_____

_____

c. Involve the stakeholders in the process. Stakeholders are those who will be affected by your plan. You need information about their needs and you need their support later for implementation.

- See pp. 10-11, *Determining Stakeholder Needs.*

d. Designate individuals to represent key groups on the planning committee (board members, management, staff, clients, etc.).

These representatives are charged with communicating to the groups they represent and collecting feedback on the draft plan from their groups. On the following page is a worksheet to help identify potential stakeholders to invite to serve on the strategic planning committee.

Planning Committee Membership

Who might represent these groups on your planning committee?

Internal Stakeholders

Clients/users _____

Leadership team _____

Board _____

Administrative support _____

Employees _____

Satellite locations _____

Donors _____

Members _____

Volunteers _____

Others _____

External Stakeholders

Elected officials _____

Service providers _____

Subcontractors _____

Community representatives _____

Advocacy groups _____

State or national chapters _____

Accrediting agencies _____

Government bodies _____

Regulatory agencies _____

Funding agencies _____

Others _____

These categories are intended to stimulate thinking. Try to keep your planning committee as small as possible while providing many opportunities for stakeholders to be engaged in the process.

e. Link the planning process to accreditation, program review, or other certification exercises.

- One option is using reaccreditation or program review and the external feedback they provide as the building blocks of a new strategic plan.

- Another option is to create or update the plan as part of the self-study process.

f. Study data from stakeholder feedback together. This can be done with the planning committee or in a staff meeting or other kind of stakeholder meeting.

This means going beyond just showing facts and figures. People need to interact with information to really grasp what it means. Ask these kinds of questions when reviewing organizational data: Where are we strong? Where are the gaps? What action is suggested?

Do you know the answers to these questions?

- Why do people give to or support our organization?

- What do our clients or partners say about us?

- What happens to clients after they use our services?

- Who competes with us? What is their appeal?

- Why do people stop giving or go elsewhere?

- In what directions are other organizations like ours moving?

- What unique benefits do we offer donors or clients?

- What do we promise? What do we not promise?

A data quiz can be a useful and lighthearted way to focus on important data points. Have planning committee members complete the quizzes in small groups with prizes for the most right answers. You will probably find very uneven knowledge of the organization among committee members.

1. What data do you have that would be useful for the planning committee to discuss?

_____

_____

_____

_____

2. What data do you need, but do not yet have, that would be useful for the planning committee to discuss?

_____

_____

_____

_____

3. How will you get the data you need but do not yet have?

_____

_____

_____

_____

Best Practice

One organization had half a dozen studies and client feedback documents. At the planning retreat, rather than telling the planning committee what these studies recommended, I divided the group into triads, with each assigned to one of the reports. After a fifteen-minute break to read the reports, the triads discussed the documents, identifying three to five key findings and what those findings suggested for the organization's future. Major points were listed on flip charts (one page only). A reporter from each group summarized. The summary sheets were posted on the wall, and participants were invited to take a "gallery walk" around the room during the next break to read them. The exercise required about sixty minutes from directions to completion of report-outs, but the information became much more meaningful to the planning committee because of their engagement with it.

g. Bring fresh air into the planning process—outside speakers, leaders from other organizations (including state or national organizations), virtual tours of other organizations' websites, lunch-hour book clubs, etc. (Outside resources can be engaged virtually via conference call or videoconferencing.)

   • It is difficult to think in new ways with the same people and the same information.

h. Look at other organizations' strategic plans (different organizations in the community or organizations like yours in other communities, states, and countries). What are the trends?

   • What other organizations' plans would it make sense for you to study?

   _____

   _____

   • Where are we ahead?

   _____

   _____

   • Where are we behind?

   _____

   _____

- Where are we in sync?

_____

_____

i. Ask, "What we can stop doing or do differently to redirect resources?" as part of the planning process.

Most organizations need to have this conversation unless they are receiving significant new sources of revenue. This can be a difficult discussion. Even when people feel overwhelmingly overworked, they can have trouble giving up activities or tasks.

One way to make this less threatening is to use these steps:

- Begin the conversation by creating criteria for "good candidates" for what could be stopped or done differently (e.g., can be done by another organization, can be done using web-based technology, can be done collaboratively with other groups, could be outsourced, will reduce paper usage, has few users, etc.)

- Brainstorm with the staff a list of things that meet these criteria for what could be stopped or done differently. (Brainstorming means no evaluative comments or criticisms until all the ideas have been listed.)

- Review and discuss the suggestions on the list. Ask these kinds of questions:

    - Who would be affected if we made the change?

    - How would stakeholders be affected?

    - What are the possible unintended consequences of changing or eliminating this process? What can we do to avoid these?

- Prioritize the possibilities and determine who has the authority to make changes.

- Those with authority to make the decision to stop doing something or do things very differently must then make those decisions using the input from the staff. Who will make the decisions and by when should be very clear.

j. Have a plan website, blog, or social networking site that includes outcomes of all meetings and input sessions, supporting documents, names of planning committee members (so people can contact them), calendar of events, timeline, etc. This helps create a transparent process and can reduce rumors and anxiety.

k. Hold formal hearings, informal review sessions, or web-based sessions on the proposed plan to ask these questions:

  • What do you like about the proposed plan and would not want to see changed?

  • What causes you concern?

  • What did we miss?

  Avoid simply asking for comments on the plan. Without a question structure, you are likely to get such wide-ranging responses that the input will be difficult to analyze and synthesize.

l. Divide up the duties for hosting various feedback sessions among the planning committee members. Not everyone has to be at every event.

  • Remind everyone involved in garnering feedback on the plan that you will be looking for patterns in the responses. Not every individual comment will result in a change.

m. Keep things moving and efficient so people don't get so tired out with creating the plan that they don't have energy to implement. Try to complete the process in three to six months from start to finish.

  What is an ideal start date for your planning process?

  _____

  When is an ideal date to have the plan approved and ready to implement?

  _____

n. Reinvigorate an existing plan. Hold an event where people in the organization can discuss these questions:

  • What does the plan mean for the work we do in our department or section?

- What action steps are needed to implement?

  See pp. 29-33 for Tree Diagrams and Gantt charts.

- What resources will we need for implementation (technology, policies, staff time, information, meetings with other entities, etc.)?

- With what groups or individuals should we partner?

"To do" on the process of creating a plan

_____

_____

_____

_____

_____

_____

_____

Engaging People in the Planning Process

A top leader once told me that he didn't believe that strategic planning worked. He described how much time he had spent creating a plan and explaining the rationales for why certain goals were important. He shared his disappointment at how little interest people showed in the plan and how "underwhelmed" he had been with the results of strategic planning. "No one did anything differently," he said. His blunt assessment was that strategic planning doesn't work.

My own assessment is different. I would say that the plan-from-above approach this leader described does not work very well. It is like walking into a movie late. You never fully "get" the movie.

In strategic planning, the process is as important as the product. A collaborative process brings more information to the table. Equally important, engagement in the process helps ensure that people understand the plan and, as a result, are more willing to implement it. Involving people (staff and clients) in the planning process is not a matter of being charitable. It is essential for implementation.

Let's say that a planning committee representing the entire organization is convened. This planning committee develops the proposed plan in a retreat through a facilitated process. How can everyone be involved directly or indirectly? These are five approaches that may be used:

1. Hold a World Café event during which a large group of staff and stakeholders can begin identifying issues essential to the future of the organization. The summary of the World Café discussions can be used as a starting point in the planning retreat. See *World Café: Magic for Involving People* on pp.11-12.

2. Survey the entire organization (web-based survey), including board members and clients, prior to the strategic planning event regarding strengths to capitalize on, weaknesses to overcome, opportunities to seize, and threats to avoid by being proactive (SWOT Analysis).

3. Hold focus groups or listening sessions for staff members to identify their needs and bring to the surface the internal and external issues affecting them, their work, and the future of the organization. See pp. 13-17.

4. Present the proposed plan to the entire staff for feedback and revision via website, e-mail, all-hands meetings, and/or informal brown bag or listening sessions.

5. Involve a variety of people in work teams to refine and carry out the broad goals identified in the strategic planning process. Ask people to indicate which goals they are interested in working on. Many people can serve on work teams who were not members of the planning committee.

Determining Stakeholder Needs

One of the elements of effective strategic planning is focused attention to the needs of stakeholders, i.e. those who will be affected by your plan. (They have a stake in the organization.) Stakeholders include employees, board members, members, clients, volunteers, donors, service providers, subcontractors, students, community employers, and the like. Other organizations with purposes similar to yours also have a stake in what direction you choose. Figuring out which are the most essential stakeholders can be a challenge. That is why I like to offer very inclusive events in which many can participate as part of the process.

Following are some practical ways to involve those we exist to serve in the planning process, with the goal of determining their needs.

1. Include several key external stakeholders on the strategic planning committee. Representatives who are not staff or board members will bring fresh insights and valuable feedback to the planning process.

2. Identify, collect, and use existing data, such as client follow-up reports or member satisfaction surveys to inform the planning process. These gold mines of information are often forgotten.

3. Hold focus groups, listening sessions, or a World Café of key stakeholders prior to the major planning event to determine their needs. Such sessions provide insight into the thinking of people who use our services or products. The information generated from the focus groups or listening sessions is valuable for situational analysis. This information can also help identify where gaps exist between the current situation and the organization's vision for itself in the future. A focus group or listening session may provide the basis for a survey.

4. Circulate the proposed strategic plan to external stakeholders for review and comment. Ask "What do you like about the proposed plan? What causes you concern? Did we miss anything?" The planning committee will be looking for patterns in responses and need not respond to every disagreement.

5. When the needs and wants of stakeholders conflict, refer back to the organization's fundamental mission (purpose). Which activities or directions are most likely to enable the organization to fulfill its purpose? Another way to reconcile competing stakeholder expectations is to reach a very clear understanding of who is asking for what. Then make choices according to criteria such as potential volume of interactions with stakeholder groups, how central stakeholder groups are within the client mix, statutory requirements, etc.

World Café: Magic for Involving People

You know the scenario. An all-hands meeting is called to discuss the strategic plan or a topic that everyone should know about. The leader dutifully shows a PowerPoint and asks if there are any questions. After a few seconds of thudding silence, one person makes a comment or asks a question. The vast majority of people do not participate. These kinds of meetings are a waste of everyone's time.

The World Café is a technique for really engaging people in questions and issues that matter to them. It uses doodling, drawing, or writing on the table, followed by discussion and the opportunity to move to a different table with a different question and another round of writing, drawing, and discussion.

I have been having great success with the World Café as a technique for really engaging people in issues that matter to them and to their organizations. In the World Café, participants sit at tables that are covered with paper. A "table host" welcomes participants and asks them to introduce themselves. They are invited to write or draw their answers to a focus question that is posted on the table. After a five to seven minute segment for thinking, writing, and drawing, the table host invites people to share their responses. Everyone looks at what is drawn or written on the table and listens for themes or connections. After fifteen to thirty minutes (depending on the questions), people move to different tables with different questions posted. (Each participant goes to a different table.) The table host remains.

In the second round, the table host again leads introductions and participants look at what the prior group wrote or drew on the table. Additions, arrows, comments, and the like are added, and the conversation continues.

A third round usually occurs, which is similar to round two except that after a brief discussion, participants help the table host prepare a list of themes and also identify any clear differences of opinion. Each table host briefly reports on themes heard.

I have used the World Café to start a strategic planning process, asking questions such as "What changes are occurring outside of our organization that we need to be aware of as we plan for the future?" or "What are some ways we can harness the energy of social networking technologies in our work?"

I have also used the World Café as a means of reviewing a draft plan and as a way to help people better understand an existing plan. Suitable questions for these purposes were "How do the three priorities in the plan relate to what is already going on?" and "What new skills do you think you or others will need to make these goals a reality?"

I like to make the atmosphere as café-like as possible, with coffee mugs to hold markers, vases of silk flowers, colorful placemats, and restaurant menu-holders for the focus question. Of course, French café music is playing as people walk in.

The World Café has much to recommend it. First, it is a friendly conversation. The questions themselves are interesting. Full participation is built in. Everyone's point of view is welcomed, regardless of job title or demographic. Different modalities are tapped —writing, drawing, speaking, and listening. Participants are asked to synthesize and look for patterns, which requires higher-order thinking than just generating ideas.

Sometimes the drawings left on the tables are zany. Sometimes they are just stick figures. Sometimes the artwork is breathtaking. The words and artwork can be photographed and made into a montage that makes a great cover for a report on the event. The World Café is the 1995 creation of a global interdisciplinary group Capital Pioneers. "Awakening and engaging collective intelligence through conversations about questions that matter" is the motto. Juanita Brown and David Isaacs have written a comprehensive "how-to" book covering the seven design principles and more: *The World Café: Shaping Our Futures Through Conversations That Matter* (2005). The helpful (and artful) website is http://www.theworldcafe.com/.

I really like the World Café approach because everyone has a chance to be part of the conversation. (One of the seven design principles for the World Café is that people should have fun.) Viewpoints that would never see the light of day in an unstructured meeting are discussed. Points of agreement are found where people thought there were none. Participants leave better educated about the issues, knowing more people in their workplace, and better able to execute organizational strategies because they have a deeper understanding of what the strategies mean. There's nothing like shared meaning to inspire people to do their best work.

Listening Session or Focus Group?

The terms "listening session" and "focus group" are used interchangeably. Is there really any difference? Based on my own observations, they are very similar activities in that both are aimed at eliciting the thoughts, ideas, feelings, and experiences of stakeholders. I see two differences—size and composition.

Focus groups are a staple of market research. The traditional focus group consists of eight to ten individuals selected because they represent an identifiable group of users or customers. For example, a large nonprofit group may want to know more about how area baby boomers decide on volunteer activities in which to participate. The focus group sponsor may purposely target people in that age group who are already active in the community.

A focus group is small enough that the facilitator can really probe answers with questions like "Can you give me an example of that? What did you wish would have happened? How would you like to see it?" A smaller group provides more opportunity for this.

A focus group moderator may take a straw poll or ask if others have similar feelings or have had similar experiences. No attempt, however, is made to get participants to agree or come to consensus.

Because participation in a focus group is voluntary and the groups are small, the people who show up are not a random sample of customers. The best one can do to get close to a balanced cross-section is to randomize the list of invitees. Focus group participants are often compensated with cash or gifts or gift certificates.

The purpose of a focus group is to listen to customers or users. Education or promotion of new products is not the purpose, although sometimes new products are introduced after a focus group has concluded.

Because focus groups are not a random sample, focus group findings cannot automatically be generalized to the whole group of users or customers. However, the focus group does provide valuable insight into how the customers think and what issues are of concern, at least to that group. In my own experience, focus group participants bring up problems that the sponsor would never have dreamed of. They make connections that are not immediately apparent.

In short, a focus group offers a look into the thinking processes of customers and offers opportunities to better align products and services with needs and contemporary lifestyles. A survey sent to a random sample of users or clients is an excellent follow-up to test out issues, problems, wants, and needs that have been raised in the focus groups. The random survey can also help determine what demographics the focus group's findings apply to most closely.

Listening sessions have become common in government and public life. These tend to be open invitations to anyone who wishes to come and express an opinion. Sometimes the sponsoring agency will provide prompt questions on pressing issues, but there is almost always unstructured time available for people in attendance to discuss anything that's on their minds. As with focus groups, no attempt is made to come to agreement or consensus in a listening session.

Numbers in listening sessions can be quite large. We are talking up to fifty people, compared to the ideal focus group number of eight to ten. Listening session participants are usually not compensated.

Open invitation listening sessions can attract a proportion of people with grievances that have not been resolved elsewhere. Thus, a thorough process for inviting and confirming the attendance of a variety of people will help generate more balanced input.

In practice, organizations may host events that exhibit aspects of both focus groups and listening sessions. For example, a nonprofit may hold listening sessions just for volunteers (like a focus group) but allow larger groups of twenty per event (like a listening session).

These are some suggestions for making focus groups or listening sessions worth everyone's time.

1. Invite twice as many people as you hope will attend.

2. Send a confirmation letter or e-mail and also a reminder postcard, letter or e-mail. A reminder phone call is ideal. Fall-off from the original number of respondents is the norm.

3. Be clear on the purpose of the focus group or listening session, both in the invitation and at the actual event. ("We are gathering members' thoughts on X in preparation for our strategic planning retreat next month.")

4. Consider using free online event ticketing sites to register participants. These sites make it easy to send follow-up communication and stay in contact with those who have signed up to attend. This approach is useful when you have

multiple sessions to track and are sure potential participants have online communication capacity.

5. Provide what your organization can afford in terms of beverages and snacks or a meal. Providing even simple refreshments like cookies, coffee, and tea sends a positive message and is appreciated by participants.

6. Select locations and times that are optimally convenient for participants. The nine to five workday may be most convenient for the organization's staff, but not so for other people who might attend. Think about access as well. The main building or location may not be the most convenient for participants.

7. Use professional facilitators or moderators, who will create a safe and friendly atmosphere that will encourage everyone to participate and who can deal with those who might attempt to dominate with their issue.

8. If professional facilitators are not possible, provide training to internal facilitators. The most important thing for internal facilitators to remember is that their role is to listen (not defend or argue) and ensure that everyone participates. Select facilitators who can create a friendly and welcoming atmosphere.

9. Designate recorders for all sessions whose role is to write down exactly what people say. These transcripts can be analyzed with qualitative data software or by hand. Create a recording template for all recorders to use. See p. 17.

10. Create or provide ground rules up front to help avoid unproductive behavior during the session. Ground rules might include items like "Allow people to finish what they are saying" or "Be brief" or "All ideas are welcome." Be clear on confidentiality assurances.

11. Create questions that are open-ended and exploratory. (Avoid "yes" or "no" questions.) Use clear language that is free of jargon and spell out any acronyms. I like to send the questions ahead so people can be thinking about them before they arrive.

12. Test the questions you will be asking with at least three people who are similar to the types of people you are inviting. Ask them how they would answer the questions and which questions, if any, were confusing to them. One or two words in a question can make a huge difference in the quality of responses.

13. Avoid having too many questions. Four questions is plenty for a one-hour session. (Depending on the group, you may have additional questions prepared to ask if those present are not able to respond to the main questions.)

14. Thank people warmly at the beginning and the end of the session. Their time and engagement is a gift (even if you aren't happy about everything you hear in the session).

15. Provide opportunities for participants to briefly talk to each other, discussing the questions first in trios and then sharing with the larger group. This will help everyone get engaged.

16. Send a follow-up thank you note or message and indicate what is happening with the results. (In listening sessions where open invitations have been made, send around a sign-up sheet for those who wish to be notified of results.) Summaries of themes should be posted on the strategic planning website.

Recording Template

Recorder: _____   Phone: _____

E-mail: _____

Session Date: _____   Location: _____

Beginning Time: _____   Ending Time: _____

Participant names:

Question 1. What attracted you to become a volunteer for XYZ?

Question 2. Describe the best experience you ever had as a volunteer for XYZ. What made that experience so special?

Question 3. What challenges do you face in being a volunteer for XYZ?

Question 4. What would make volunteering for XYZ an even better experience for you?

Figure 2. Template for Recording Listening Sessions

2.   Evaluating the Plan

Look at your proposed plan in light of the following questions:

a. The plan should have both a longer-term visionary and strategic component (three to five years) and annual or short-term objectives. Does your plan have both?

b. Is the list of longer-term strategic priorities "doable" in the timeframe?

   • The list of priorities should be short enough to easily remember.

c. The plan is a contract between the leader and the organization. The contract commitment is that the leader will provide resources to accomplish the stated goals, and everyone else will do his or her part to achieve the stated goals. Is the plan viewed as a contract?

   • Anything that is not really feasible should be deleted.

d. Are the goals "SMART"?

   • **S**pecific

   • **M**easurable

   • **A**ctionable

   • **R**ealistic

   • **T**ime bound

   See Figure 8, Action Planning Format on p. 36.

e. Are the organizational goals *really* goals for the whole enterprise, or has someone's "to do" list taken over?

f. Does the plan show how and where it's aligned with the larger entity of which it is a part? For example, a statewide organization may be part of a national or international organization that has its own plan. Showing clearly where the state plan aligns with the national plan can give the state plan increased credibility and focus, and may even attract additional resources.

    • The alignment doesn't have to be perfect.

g. Use the free Wordle™ software at http://www.wordle.net/ to create "word clouds" that will help you analyze which words, phrases, concepts appear most frequently in your plan. Are they the ones you want to have center stage?

h. When will the plan be officially adopted by the board or decision-making body?

i. Do some of the "measures of success" measure impact? An example of an impact measure is "All employees use the new system with an average of less than .001 percent errors" versus "All employees are trained on the new system." Impact measures are typically more difficult to measure than simple counts of activity, but a few impact measures are likely to be more valuable than many counts of activities.

j. As a rule of thumb, only collect measures that, if they change, will prompt action. Eliminating reports and data collection that are not useful or used is one way to free up organizational resources to focus on the plan.

"To do" for evaluating the plan

_____

_____

_____

_____

_____

3. Communicating the Plan

a. Post the plan where people can easily find it (home page, one-pagers, flyers, posters, etc.).

- Where is our strategic plan now? _____

b. Create several different versions for different audiences (staff, potential members, accrediting bodies, recruitment, etc.).

- Staff who will implement the plan need more detail than external readers.

- A one-page version or brochure is essential (mission, vision, strategic priorities). This is useful for staff recruitment as well as pubic information.

c. Make the document look as appealing as your resources allow.

- Fancy packaging won't do much for a poor plan, but poor packaging can detract from a good plan.

What users or target audiences might need different versions of your strategic plan?

_____

_____

d. Consider the stakeholders and members of the public who should know about the plan. Create a matrix showing what strategies will be used to inform which groups. See sample on p. 23.

e. Give the plan an inspiring name (*Connecting for Success, Innovations for Kids, New Paths, The Parkside Promise, Three by Thirteen,* etc.).

f. Champion the priorities of the organization in public speaking opportunities whenever possible. Create online "kits" for everyone who addresses outside groups, stocked with handouts, audio-visual presentations, giveaways, and anything else that helps people understand your priorities.

g. Publish annual updates on plan progress. Use charts, graphs, and visual representations of progress whenever possible. Find ideas for graphically reporting in "A Periodic Table of Visualization Methods," which includes examples from bar charts to radar charts to "Heaven and Hell" maps. See http://www.visual-literacy.org/.

h. Create a one-page strategy map as described by authors Kaplan and Norton.[3] In a strategy map, the organization's strategic priorities are shown as "bubbles" arranged according to the Balanced Scorecard domains of Customer, Finances, Internal, and Learning and Growth (people). The strategy map can help illuminate the underlying assumptions and how the priorities are connected.

"To do" for communicating the plan

_____

_____

_____

_____

_____

_____

_____

---

3 Robert S. Kaplan and David C. Norton, *The Strategy-Focused Organization: How the Balanced Scorecard Companies Thrive in the New Business Environment* (Boston: Harvard Business School Publishing Corporation, 2001), 69-105.

<u>Communications Strategies for the New Plan</u>

Stakeholder Groups	Best Way to Communicate With Them
Clients/users	
Leadership team	
Board	
All employees	
Satellite locations	
Donors	
Members	
Volunteers	
Service providers and subcontractors	
Community representatives	
Advocacy groups	
State or national chapters	
Accrediting agencies	
Government bodies	
Elected officials	
Regulatory agencies	
Funding agencies	
Others	

Figure 3. Target Constituencies for a Communications Plan

4. Implementing the Plan

a. Identify a point person for each strategic priority and goal—someone who makes sure the goal is moving forward, connects people who are working on it, and reports on progress.

   • The point can be a committee, but the chair of the committee should be listed as the point person.

   • The point person does not necessarily have to have functional authority over those implementing.

   • See p. 28, *The Point Person Makes All The Difference.*

b. Break down big goals into manageable pieces.

   • Create (or request) a thirty-day or sixty-day implementation plan to create immediate action.

      or

   • Identify a launching step for each goal (see p. 36).

   • Create Tree Diagrams (see p. 31) to show the big steps and the smaller supporting activities.

   • Create Gantt charts (see pp. 32-33) to identify responsibilities and timeline.

c. Use existing structures as much as possible for implementation and avoid creating new committees or task forces.

- Every new department, committee, or executive position will consume additional organizational resources just to maintain itself. Consider shoring up existing areas where responsibility rests with additional resources before creating new entities.

d. Structure regular staff meetings around individual priorities or goals to provide time to focus.

- Set up a schedule at the start of the planning year (see p. 35).

e. Provide progress reports to the whole organization at least once a year. Top leadership needs more frequent progress checks, either monthly or quarterly.

- See *Check Meetings,* p. 34.

f. Show progress toward goals visually (charts, graphs, maps, etc.).

g. Link the plan to performance reports or activity reports.

- Use the plan to help set individual performance goals.

- Use the plan to structure how people report what they are doing.

h. Use the plan to make professional development decisions.

i. Designate someone besides the CEO to be the point person for the planning process overall, ensuring that "check meetings" are held and that time is made available for planning work.

j. Use the plan to guide budget requests and decisions.

k. Look for the low-hanging fruit, those changes that can be made immediately with relatively little time and effort. Early, effective action goes a long way to building credibility for the implementation process.

l. Celebrate milestones accomplished!

Best Practice

At St. Mary's Hospital, Madison, Wisconsin, SSM Healthcare:

- **Every** department displays posters showing how it supports that hospital's plan.

- **All** employees, including physicians, have "passports" describing what they will do personally in the next year to implement their department's plan.

"To do" for implementing the plan

_____

_____

_____

_____

_____

_____

_____

The Point Person Makes All the Difference

As a planning consultant, I have seen a lot of plans for both large and small organizations. I cannot always predict which ones will be successful, which ones will light up the sky and take the organization to new levels. I can, however, always predict the plans that are destined to go nowhere. What tells me these ill-fated plans will never be implemented? It is the absence of point people. We should find a point person wherever there is a goal or some kind of collective action taking place.

A point person is not quite the same thing as the team leader, although one could serve both functions, depending on the situation. A team leader often has some functional authority over those working on a particular effort or has authority "bestowed" for the task. But what about efforts that involve players from different parts of the organization, who ordinarily may interact very little, and perhaps hold varying levels of authority and responsibility? These horizontal efforts can benefit by having a point person.

The point person is responsible for ensuring that the goal is progressing as planned. Without functional authority over many or any of the players, the point person's tools are progress checks, documentation, and dissemination of what has been accomplished. The point person also is the only one with the "view of the whole" and connection to all the parts, and thus plays an essential linking role, connecting people with others whose efforts are related. This perspective on both the parts and the whole makes the point person uniquely situated for coordinating reporting of progress and results.

In any organization, it can be difficult to know who to go to. The point person is that "go to" person, the individual whom people can go to with ideas for improvement, concerns, or to identify an opportunity that the group might seize.

If a group's progress toward a goal is blocked, the point person takes the initiative to work with the group to resolve the problem and move forward.

The point person should spend some time thinking about what parts of the organization he or she will be interacting with to ensure momentum. A conversation with the individual(s) responsible for those areas sooner rather than later is advisable to avoid unnecessary conflict and misunderstandings. The conversation can center on who should be contacted, times to avoid, existing committees and structures, expectations, and so on. The point person will need to initiate these conversations periodically.

Without point people, goals in even the best strategic plans can languish. With a point person, someone is clearly responsible for nurturing the goal along.

Using Self-Stick Notes to Create Tree Diagrams and Gantt Charts

When an exciting "stretch" goal has been agreed upon, those charged with implementation may feel overwhelmed. It can be difficult to know where or how to begin.

Two tools from quality improvement are extremely helpful in clarifying implementation steps: Tree Diagrams and Gantt charts. The Tree Diagram (see p. 31) is one of the seven "management and planning tools" described by Michael Brassard.[4] It is a "picture" of the tasks that must be accomplished and resembles a tree on its side. The trunk represents the main goal, the branches represent large sub goals and the twigs and leaves represent objectives or tasks. The Gantt chart, named for its designer Henry L. Gantt (1861–1919), is a calendar-based bar chart showing when activities begin and end within a project.

The approach to creating Tree Diagrams and Gantt charts described here is the old-fashioned approach (without software). I think the process of manually writing the items on self-stick notes and manipulating them create more buy-in and understanding than a perfectly rendered software diagram. The process really is as important as the product. Microsoft Excel, however, can create both of these charts for you.

Tree Diagram

Both Tree Diagrams and Gantt charts begin with a brainstorm using self-stick or Post-It™ notes. You will need one main color and a smaller number of notes of a different color. Be clear on what the ultimate goal is—creating an event, offering a new service, adopting a new technology, etc. I write the goal on a piece of paper on the table or work surface. This goal forms the trunk of the Tree Diagram.

Invite those involved in implementation to silently write on the self-stick notes every step, task, and concern, they can think of that is necessary to achieve the goal (one item per note). After about five minutes, cluster everyone's notes into groupings that are similar. For example, all the notes regarding information meetings, the website, and brochure items would probably be clustered together.

You will find that you have several clusters. Place a different-colored note atop each cluster, with a heading name such as Communication, Benchmarking, Training, Needs Assessment, Programming, Funding, etc. This exercise can be done by one individual, but a small group working together will be more thorough.

---

4 Michael Brassard, The Memory Jogger Plus+ (Salem, NH: GOAL/QPC, 1996), 73-98.

Place the clusters in a vertical line to the right of the "trunk." The titles on each cluster are most likely the branches for your Tree Diagram.

Look again at the notes within each cluster. Each required action is a leaf. Lay the individual notes in a vertical line on the right side of each branch. You may need to create some new "leaf" notes to cover all the action that will be required.

Any notes that are duplicates or determined not to be necessary can be grouped in a recycle pile. If someone has written a concern or possible unintended consequence, discuss and create a leaf (action item) that addresses the concern. The action item might be special communications or purchases or may be as simple as monitoring for signs of problems. Identifying these possible unintended consequences early on will save time and energy later.

Once all the "leaf" notes have been checked over and determined to be important, the next question is "If we do all these things, will we achieve the "branch" goal or activity? Similarly, if we complete all these 'branch' activities, will we reach our 'trunk' goal?" The completed Tree Diagram will look like a tree lying horizontally (see Figure 4).

Gantt Chart

The Gantt chart is essentially a calendar (see pp. 32-33). The same self-stick "leaf" notes can be arranged in sequence starting with what needs to happen first. Write on the note when a particular activity will begin and when it should be completed. Identify who will be responsible for ensuring completion.

The information on the self-stick notes can then be transferred to a Gantt chart (see Figure 6). Milestones or special deadlines may be highlighted with colors or symbols.

In summary, thinking and talking together about all the implementation steps for a goal or project and then creating a visual representation through a Tree Diagram or Gantt chart can help groups move forward with increased clarity and confidence.

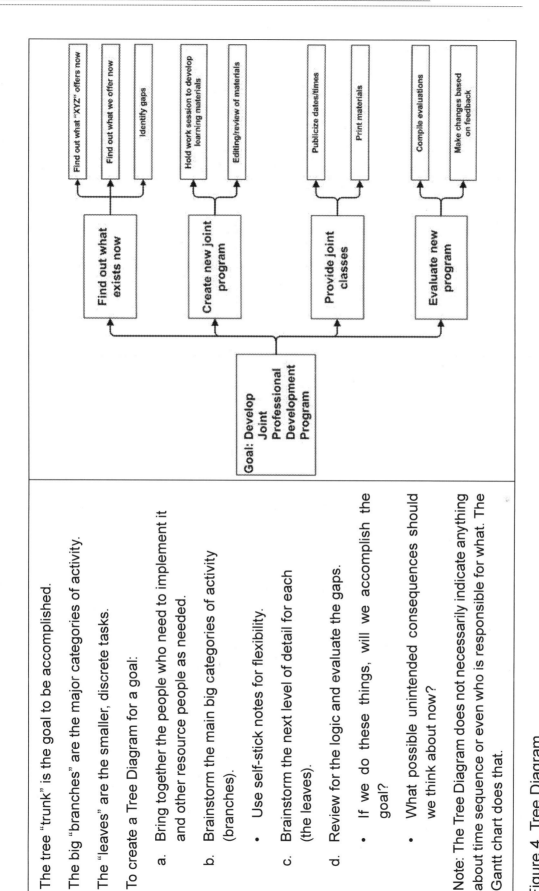

The tree "trunk" is the goal to be accomplished.

The big "branches" are the major categories of activity.

The "leaves" are the smaller, discrete tasks.

To create a Tree Diagram for a goal:

a. Bring together the people who need to implement it and other resource people as needed.

b. Brainstorm the main big categories of activity (branches).

- Use self-stick notes for flexibility.

c. Brainstorm the next level of detail for each (the leaves).

d. Review for the logic and evaluate the gaps.

- If we do these things, will we accomplish the goal?

- What possible unintended consequences should we think about now?

Note: The Tree Diagram does not necessarily indicate anything about time sequence or even who is responsible for what. The Gantt chart does that.

Figure 4. Tree Diagram

Gantt Chart for a Strategic Planning Process

Action	Who	Aug	Sep	Oct	Nov	Dec	Jan	Feb	Mar	Apr	May
Finalize process and timeline	HP	X									
Appoint a planning committee and set up meeting schedule	HP	X									
Appoint a person to lead the effort	DT	X									
Engage an external consultant/facilitator	DT	X									
Set up a website or other information channel that is used throughout the process	RJ	X	X	X	X	X	X				
Develop a communications plan and begin to communicate internally and externally	CC	X	X	X	X	X	X				
Design ways to engage people: focus groups, dialogue sessions, e-mail lists, World Cafés, web links	CC	X	X	X	X	X	X				
Gather information for environmental scan and SWOT analysis	CC	X	X								
Retreat for steering committee to create draft plan	CC	X	X	X							
Review of draft by stakeholders				X	X						
Refinement of draft based on feedback					X	X					
Presentation to Board						X	X				

Figure 5. Gantt Chart for a Strategic Planning Process

Gantt Chart

Goals and Actions	Who*										

*The "Who" is the "point person" who makes sure the goal is progressing and that people with assignments are completing them. The point person reports on progress and is the "go to" person for ideas and coordination of activities. The point person does not do all the work!

Figure 6. Blank Gantt Chart

Check Meetings

When I am working with a group to create goals, I like to set a date and time to check on progress right then and there. Any group needs all the help it can get to stay on target.

Some groups designate regular meeting times as their check dates. For example, "We will check on Goal #1 at the September staff meeting, Goal #2 at the October staff meeting, etc." Calendars are created to show which staff meetings will focus on what goals (see Figure 7).

Other groups have quarterly or semiannual meetings devoted to checking on plan progress. Either of these approaches (staff meetings or special meetings) can work well if the group is vigilant about really utilizing the time for checking progress. In either case, an annual meeting to update and refresh the overall plan is necessary.

Check meetings achieve multiple purposes. They bring everyone up to speed on progress and show where various initiatives connect. Check meetings also illuminate problems, such as blocked progress or overlap. People should leave the meeting with a clear understanding of the next steps and their responsibilities, as well as confidence that the plan is moving forward.

As a rule of thumb, check meetings should cover these four areas:

1. Purpose for meeting

2. Action to date: Successes, barriers, sticking points

3. Strategies to get over, around or through the barriers/sticking points

4. Upcoming deadlines (on assignments, due dates)

I would not recommend having a face-to-face check meeting solely to report on progress. That can be done via e-mail or a conference call. Rather, use the check meeting partially to report on progress, but more importantly, to get at the things that are blocking progress and strategize together how to get over, around, or through them to keep the goals moving.

Staff Meeting Check Dates for Strategic Plan

February 8

How are we doing on Goal A (Improve communication between administration and work groups)?

Point Person: Julie

February 22

How are we doing on Goal B (Creating self service options)?

Point Person: Bernie

March 8

How are we doing on Goal C (Events scheduling to avoid conflicts)?

Point Person: Candice

March 22

How are we doing on Goal D (Partner with state agencies)?

Point Person: Tom

April 5

How are we doing on Goal E (Expand services in eastern counties)?

Point Person: Sharrone

April 19

How are we doing on Goal F (Going paperless)?

Point Person: Holly

May 3

Review strategic plan goals for the year.

Point Person: Asst. Director

- What should we be doing over the summer to move the plan forward?

Figure 7. Staff Meeting Check Dates for a Strategic Plan

Action Planning Format

Strategic Priority:

_____

Goal:

_____

Point Person:

_____

#	Action Steps	Point Person	Involved (internal)	Involved (external)	Measure (s) Indicators of Success	Done (X)
1.	30-day launching step:					
2.						
3.						
4.						
5.						

Figure 8. Action Planning Format

Goals for action planning should be reviewed and revised each year, with new goals replacing those that have been accomplished.

If it is necessary to assign someone to a task when he or she is not present, indicate who will discuss the needed activities with the individual and by what date.

Using a Dashboard to Monitor Implementation

Visual representations of information are more powerful than words alone. The sample dashboard below tracks individual goals, which are arranged by strategic priority. Each organization can decide for itself which goals or initiatives should appear on the dashboard. Too much detail can make a dashboard cluttered, unappealing, and easy to ignore. Use the actual colors indicated if possible. Shading is used here. Green is progress; yellow is caution; and red is warning: there's a problem or issue that requires attention.

Strategic Plan Goals/Projects	Schedule	Budget	Quality	Scope	Comments
A. Expand Partnerships (Point Person: John Q.)					
A1. Offer a patient seminar series in collaboration with XYQ (Sally M.)	Green	Yellow	Green	Green	50 participants. Costs were $200 more than budgeted for.
A2. Submit one proposal for funding jointly with another nonprofit for no less than $10,000 (Lan N.)	Green	Green	Red	Red	Only $5000, but we got the grant by applying with the ABC NGO.
B. Increase earned revenue to $100,000 annually (Point Person: Marge L.)					
B1. Increase sales of our annual art poster (Pete V.)	Yellow	Green	Yellow	Yellow	Contacts made with all 10 area bookstores, no orders yet.
B2. Charge for support group topics offered online (Ann Z.)	Red	Red	Red	Red	Nothing has been done on this. Counselors need technical help.

Figure 9. Implementation Dashboard

Making the Priorities Personal

Every employee should have a direct line of sight between his or her work and the organization's top priorities. This cannot happen without a purposeful effort on the part of leadership. Below is a summary of strategies discussed throughout this document that will help to create that line of sight.

1. Ensure that the plan identifies priorities or focus areas. If the plan reads like poetry and nothing stands out as more important than anything else, members of the organization cannot shape their work around it.

2. Hold a conversation or World Café (see pp. 11-12) within each office, department, and unit of the organization about plan priorities. Questions can include:

   - How do the priorities in the plan relate to our work?

   - What are we doing now that supports these priorities?

   - What other actions can we take in this office/department/unit to achieve these goals or support the priorities?

   - What new skills do you think you or others will need to make these goals a reality?

   - What resources will we need?

   - How will we know we are making progress?

3. Ask employees to set their annual performance goals according to the priorities. (Some priorities will not fit as well as others in any given unit.) Evaluate annual performance accordingly.

   - In one college, a top priority was retention of first-year students. The maintenance staff at first thought they had no role to play in this priority, but after discussion, members decided that they had a role in making the campus as welcoming as possible. Goals they came up with focused on improved signage and more aggressive trash removal in certain campus areas, both of which had been identified as student complaints. They also agreed that they would drop whatever they were doing to help students and guests who appeared to be lost. The first two goals—signage and trash removal—are measurable. The third will be difficult to measure beyond anecdotal reports, but still very much worth doing.

4. Require all requests for professional development funds to indicate how that activity supports the priorities. Rank requests and make decisions about professional development fund allocation based on relationship to priorities. (In most cases, a new plan will require people to develop new skills.)

   Beyond conferences and workshops, professional development can include books, DVDs, downloads, online learning, opportunities to shadow in other parts of the organization, benchmarking with other organizations, writing and submitting articles for professional journals, etc. These options can be discussed as part of the employee performance appraisal process.

5. Discuss their position descriptions with all employees. Are they accurate? What duties need to change in light of the plan priorities?

6. Make the vision or priorities visible in as many ways as possible (posters, mugs, screen savers, mouse pads, e-mail signatures, business cards, etc.).

   - Visitors and employees who walk into the main office of the Wisconsin Historical Society Foundation in Madison, Wisconsin, see a huge, framed poster of the organization's values and plan priorities.

7. Reward and thank employees who put extra effort into strategic priorities. Rewards can be significant or modest, based on the organization's capacity. Besides formal recognition or awards, consider movie tickets, books, gift certificates, flowers, thank you notes, cookies, dining out, etc.

   - Be specific when thanking people. Rather than "Thanks for your work," say something like, "Thanks for everything you did to plan and publicize the Volunteer Appreciation Golf Outing. We had a record turnout thanks to you."

Your ideas for making the plan personal:

_____

_____

_____

_____

_____

5. Budgeting for the Plan

The strategic plan should be approved before the next cycle of budget planning is completed to ensure that the budget follows the plan rather than vice versa. Even brilliant professionals can forget to link their strategic plans to their budgets. (Note that not all consultants agree with this advice, but I think it's a logical sequence.)

Some organizations, faced with shrinking budgets, decline to plan strategically. They hunker down and try to keep doing what they have always done. This approach ensures that no innovation, new services, or new partnerships will be created that might strengthen the organization's financial position. It allows worn-out processes that may have outlived their purpose to continue unexamined. Deciding not to plan because of budget cuts is a mistake because it ignores this fact: a good plan is a resource attractor. A plan that shows clear direction and focus can attract funds through grants, donors, and partners. An organization without a focus is not an attractive investment for anyone.

Finally, our time is our most precious resource. Any organization needs to be sure that people are focusing their time and energy on the most strategic activities. Without a plan, people will still find plenty of things to do, but all those "things to do" may not ultimately make a difference for the organization.

Even with the most ideal planning and budgeting cycle, some sectors of an organization are going to get fewer resources than they feel they need or should have. The planning and budgeting approach described here is transparent, and at the very least, people will know why certain priorities received funds while others did not.

Ask for goals first, budget line items second. It is irresponsible for a leader to allocate financial resources to a unit or department that lacks a credible plan. The planning and budgeting approach shown on p. 45 requires every unit to do some planning for

41

the next two to five years in light of the organization's strategic priorities. Using this or a similar format will help ensure that the budget decision process does not have a life of its own and is, rather, a means of achieving the organization's aims.

Beyond *Program Plans and Budget Requests,* every organization must figure out how its current approaches to budgeting need to change to better align resources in support of the plan. For example, an organization that is using zero-based budgeting should find it relatively easy to use the strategic priorities to shape budget decisions each year. (Zero-based budgeting contrasts with traditional incremental budgeting in that managers must justify the full amount of their budget request, not merely the increases. Theoretically every budget goes back to zero every budget year.) Organizations such as large hospitals with multiple sources of income and a galaxy of clinics and cost centers may find budget alignment more complicated. See "Making Budget Decisions: Aligning Resources with Priorities" at http://oqi.wisc.edu/. This document from the Office of Quality Improvement, University of Wisconsin–Madison includes questions to guide the discussion.

Suggestions for budgeting according to the plan:

a. Resist across-the-board cuts; they are antithetical to strategic planning.

b. Involve the CFO or top financial leader as part of the planning committee.

c. Initiate a dialogue among the CFO or financial director, key staff members, and the organization's top leadership team around these questions:

- What can we do to make sure that our operational budget dollars are invested in activities and positions that support our strategic priorities?

- What are the possibilities for modifying our account coding structure so we can monitor the flow of funds into priority areas or toward particular client segments?

- What changes need to occur in our current planning and budgeting processes to bring them into closer alignment (timing, sequence, labor required, duplication of information, etc.)?

- What about our capital budget? How can we bring it into closer alignment with our priorities? What should be updated?

  The capital budget covers those large infrastructure building and improvement projects that are normally funded through long-term debt in the public sector. The capital budget can get forgotten in the annual planning process, even though infrastructure can be a huge strategic advantage.

d. Make alignment of the strategic plan with the budget part of the finance director's or CFO's position description. That individual (or his or her direct report) should be affirmed for making the necessary changes and adjustments to the budget process to ensure alignment.

e. Use the strategic plan priorities to make decisions about windfall or unexpected short-term dollars that may become available.

f. Link funds with outcomes. The State of North Carolina, in its budgeting process, requires at least one stated client outcome for each budget fund. The outcome must be a result with societal value, not an activity (e.g., employment status, reduction in mortality, reduced recidivism, educational degree achievement, etc.). See "Step 9A–Connect the Strategic Plan to the Results-based Budgeting System" at http://www.performancesolutions.nc.gov/.

g. Establish criteria for making decisions about discontinuing programs and services. Criteria can be relationship to priorities, usage, demand, time required, expense, effectiveness, etc. Whatever criteria are identified, they must be used similarly throughout the organization.

h. Institute an open-book policy for budget and financial information. This transparency will help give credibility to the effort to focus resources in the strategic directions of the organization.

i. Use a 2 x 2 chart similar to the one below to help make decisions about budget or position requests. You may use different criteria, such as institutional readiness.

	High Relationship to Plan Priorities	Low Relationship to Plan Priorities
High Impact		
Low Impact		

Figure 10. 2 x 2 Chart for Budget Request Decisions

j. If the budgeting and planning cycles are out of sync (which can happen when a new leader comes on board), designate dollars in the budget for strategic priorities even before those are known or defined by the planning process. It is likely that a major portion of new funds will be for labor and enhanced technology.

k. Use mini-grants to stimulate activity and interest in the plan's strategic priorities. A small amount of resources can sometimes create a large amount of momentum. One university's very successful effort for creating residential learning communities was seeded with funds that paid for cookies, coffee, and copying for the early meetings. Establishing a small-scale success is often the key to attracting larger external funds.

"To do" for budgeting for the plan:

_____

_____

_____

_____

_____

_____

_____

Program Plans and Budget Requests

Department or Unit:	
Submitted by:	
1.	Major Accomplishments: *(Anticipated status at the end of the fiscal year. List appropriate data and/or projected accomplishments related to last year's plans.)*
2.	Strengths and Opportunities: *(What are the major strengths of the department or unit? What opportunities exist because of these strengths?)*
3.	Limitations, Barriers, Weaknesses: *(What factors limit progress? What barriers limit future development? Identify any weaknesses that should be addressed in planning for the future.)*
4.	List the 2-5 year goals for this department:
5.	*List objectives proposed for next year:*

Objective	Organizational Strategic Priorities Addressed

6.	What did you do differently this past year to conserve resources (time, dollars, energy, space, etc.)?
7.	What major changes are anticipated for the upcoming year?
8.	List new staff needed (in priority order):
9.	List new major equipment needed (in priority order, $1000 and up):
10.	List new/modified facilities needed:
11.	Identify other major changes, including activities and expenses from last year that have been deleted in this budget:

Figure 11. Planning and Budgeting Format

The budget and planning document in Figure 11 should be completed by all the offices, departments, and units within the organization during the same time period.

Aligning Your Strategic Plan Throughout the Organization

1. Ensure that position descriptions reflect reality. Modify as needed according to strategic priorities.

2. Ensure that the organizational structure is functional for creating the change you wish to see (e.g. are units combined in ways that make sense for the plan priorities?).

3. Eliminate or streamline even long-standing processes in light of new priorities.

4. Determine what information employees will need to access because of the new priorities.

5. Allocate professional development dollars based on strategic priorities.

6. Build the budget based on the plan (rather than the other way around).

7. Determine what information technology capacities your organization will need in view of the plan.

8. Evaluate leaders based on their follow-through as point people and on their implementation of the plan throughout the areas for which they are responsible.

9. Use pilot projects before full-scale changes. (A lot can be learned by smaller field tests and pilots.)

10. Set aside some seed funds (even if the amount is small) to stimulate interest in new activities.

11. Identify a point person for each priority. Each major priority needs a top leader as point person or champion. This responsibility is part of that person's job.

12. Make progress reports on the strategic plan visible and a big deal. Use graphs and charts to show progress.

13. Use strategic priorities as the template for all organizational units to report annually on activity. Share these reports widely.

14. Publicize progress and gains. See a sample annual progress report for a university, *For Wisconsin and the World: First Year Progress Report* at http://www.chancellor.wisc.edu/.

15. Use the plan for hiring. No open positions should be refilled automatically without considering the plan. Different competencies may be needed for achieving new priorities.

16. Reward and thank employees who put extra effort into strategic priorities. Rewards can be significant or modest based on the organization's capacity. Besides formal recognition or awards, movie tickets, books, gift certificates, flowers, thank you notes, cookies, and restaurant meals all have meaning.

Self-Evaluation of the Strategic Planning Process

Please answer the following questions below on a scale where 1 is "to no extent" and 5 is "to a great extent." If you don't know, leave blank.

	Questions	Your Evaluation				
1.	Does the *mission* or *purpose* concisely state what will be done, for whom, and why?	1	2	3	4	5
2.	Is the *vision* a descriptive statement of where and what the organization wants to be in the future?	1	2	3	4	5
3.	Is there evidence that employees at all levels participated in a meaningful way in planning?	1	2	3	4	5
4.	Is there evidence that data on the needs of internal stakeholders were used in the planning process?	1	2	3	4	5
5.	Is there evidence that data on the needs of external stakeholders (funding agencies, partners, government agencies, employers, etc.) were used in the planning process?	1	2	3	4	5
6.	Are goals prioritized annually or in some way?	1	2	3	4	5
7.	Are limitations, barriers, and weaknesses addressed in strategies, goals, or objectives?	1	2	3	4	5
8.	Is there evidence that planners looked beyond immediate day-to-day concerns and into the future?	1	2	3	4	5
9.	Does the plan show that *choices* have been made in terms of new activities, service delivery, who will be served, processes, etc.?	1	2	3	4	5
10.	Do plans show evidence of cooperation, collaboration, and/or integration of resources?	1	2	3	4	5
11.	Are measures of success (quantifiable outcomes) identified?	1	2	3	4	5
12.	Are measures of *impact* included?	1	2	3	4	5
13.	Is there a copy of the strategic plan (or a summary) in the hands of every full-time staff member?	1	2	3	4	5
14.	Are formal progress reports presented at least once during each year?	1	2	3	4	5

Questions	Your Evaluation				
15. When a major decision must be made (hiring, new program, etc.), is the strategic plan consulted?	1	2	3	4	5
16. Does the budget follow the plan?	1	2	3	4	5
17. For each goal or priority, is someone assigned as "point person" or given responsibility for implementation?	1	2	3	4	5
18. Is the plan linked to key HR functions (e.g. performance reviews, goal-setting, professional development)?	1	2	3	4	5

If you circled any "1" or "2" responses, what opportunities do you see for improving your planning process?

_____

_____

_____

Bibliography

Allison, Michael and Jude Kaye. 2005. *Strategic Planning for Nonprofit Organizations.* 2nd ed. Hoboken, NJ: John Wiley & Sons, Inc.

Below, Patrick J., George L. Morrissey, and Betty L. Acomb. 1987. *The Executive Guide to Strategic Planning.* San Francisco: Jossey-Bass.

Bossidy, Larry, Ram Charan, and Charles Burck. 2002. *Execution: The Discipline of Getting Things Done.* New York: Random House.

Brassard, Michael. 1996. *The Memory Jogger Plus+: Featuring the Seven Management and Planning Tools.* Salem, NH: GOAL/QPC.

Brown, Juanita and David Isaacs. 2005. *The World Café: Shaping Our Futures Through Conversations That Matter. San Francisco:* Berrett-Koehler Publishers.

Bryson, John M. 2004. *Strategic Planning for Public and Nonprofit Organizations: A Guide to Strengthening and Sustaining Organizational Achievement.* 3rd ed. San Francisco: Jossey-Bass.

Carlson, Mim and Margaret Donohoe. 2002. *The Executive Director's Survival Guide.* San Francisco: Jossey-Bass.

Eppler, Martin J. and Ralph Lengler. [n.d.]. A periodic table of visualization methods. http://www.visual-literacy.org/periodic_table/periodic_table.html.

Feinberg, Jonathan. 2009. Wordle™. http://www.wordle.net/.

Kaplan, Robert S. and David P. Norton. 2001. *The Strategy-Focused Organization: How Balanced Scorecard Companies Thrive in the New Business Environment.* Boston: Harvard Business School Publishing Corporation.

North Carolina Office of State Personnel. 2008. *Step 9A—Connect the Strategic Plan to the Results-based Budgeting System.* http://www.performancesolutions.nc.gov/.

Office of Quality Improvement, University of Wisconsin-Madison. [n.d.]. *Making Budget Decisions: Aligning Resources with Priorities.* http://quality.wisc.edu/index.htm/.

Paris, Kathleen A. 2006. *Does It Pay to Plan? What We Learned About Strategic Planning in a Big Ten University.* Madison: University of Wisconsin System Board of Regents. http://www.ncci-cu.org/go/publications?page=3/.

Plantes, Mary Kay and Robert Finfrock. 2009. *Beyond Price: Differentiate Your Company in Ways That Really Matter.* Austin, TX: Greenleaf Book Group Press.

Person, Ron. 2008. *Balanced Scorecards and Operational Dashboards with Microsoft Excel.* Indianapolis: Wiley Publishing Company.

Pullan, Penny and Vanessa Randle. 2010. *Graphics Made Easy.* http://www.graphicsmadeeasy.co.uk/.

Spencer, Laura J. 1989. *Winning Through Participation: Meeting the Challenge of Corporate Change with the Technology of Participation.* Dubuque, Iowa: Kendall/Hunt Publishing Company.

Tromp, Sherry and Brent Ruben, eds. 2004. *Strategic Planning in Higher Education: A Guide for Leaders.* Washington, D.C.: NACUBO.

Wilkinson, Michael. 2004. *The Secrets of Facilitation: The S.M.A.R.T. Guide to Getting Results with Groups.* San Francisco: Jossey-Bass.

The World Café. http://www.theworldcafe.com.

University of Wisconsin-Madison. 2010. *For Wisconsin and the World: First Year Progress Report.* http://www.chancellor.wisc.edu/.